MICROWAVE COOKING
FOR CHILDREN

Gloria

PIATKUS

For

Acknowledgements
I should like to thank:
Thorn EMI for lending me a Tricity Microwave oven model 2004T
Corning for supplying browners
Lakeland Plastics for supplying almost everything
Stewart Plastics for microwave cookware.
A special thanks to SS

© text and illustrations Gloria 1986

First published in 1986 by Judy Piatkus (Publishers) Limited,
5 Windmill Street, London W1

British Library Cataloguing in Publication Data

Gloria
   Microwave cooking for children.
   1. Microwave cookery — Juvenile literature
   I. Title
   641.5'882   TX832
   ISBN 0-86188-530-9

Phototypeset in V.I.P. Futura Book by
D. P. Media Limited, Hitchin
Printed and bound in Great Britain by
W. S. Cowell Ltd, Ipswich

the how to...

1. All recipes given are for one generous portion.
2. All recipes in this book have been tested and timed in a 650 watt oven with a turntable.
3. If you have a 500 or 600 watt oven, allow for longer cooking times. Less time is needed for ovens of 700 or 750 watts.
4. Standing time is important. Food continues to cook even after the microwave energy has been turned off. Take it out of the oven, place on a mat and allow to stand for the required length of time.
5. It is necessary to cover certain foods with a lid or cling film to retain moisture and prevent the food from drying out. The steam also helps to speed up the cooking process.
6. A tomato, sausage or potato must have its skin pierced or it will burst during cooking.
7. Browning dishes will give a conventional "fried" appearance to food. It is important to press food down hard to make contact with the special surface of the dish. Once food is turned over, however, the second side will be a far paler colour, although it will be cooked. (To achieve a brown effect on both sides you would have to clean and reheat the empty browning dish.) Do not touch browning dishes without oven gloves, and always stand them on a mat. They get very hot!
8. "KT" (kitchen towels) are referred to and used in many recipes. One sheet will form a loose cover over the food and prevent spattering on the oven walls. It is also used as a base to rest food on, such as rolls.
9. All foods used in the recipes are at room temperature (other than milk, cream, etc.). Food taken straight from the refrigerator will take slightly longer to cook.

why to... pages

Do's ... and don'ts

1. **DO** cover food only if recipe tells you to.
2. **DO** pierce the cling film with a wooden toothpick in 2 places.
3. **DO** use a new piece of cling film if the first piece has torn or become soggy.
4. **DO** cook on FULL (100%) unless recipe states otherwise.
5. **DO** stand food covered if it was cooked covered.
6. **DO** be sure that dishes required to be used in the microwave and under the conventional grill are suitable for both.
7. **DO** always wear oven gloves and use a mat with browning dishes and when the food contains a lot of fat or sugar.
8. **DO** ask for help when you see the red star.

1. **DON'T** put any metal objects in the oven.
2. **DON'T** use any utensils that are not microwave safe.
3. **DON'T** think that food isn't cooked because it isn't brown.

What do I need ... ?

1. **I NEED** to read the recipe and get everything ready before I start.
2. **I NEED** cling film to cover food.
3. **I NEED** wooden toothpicks to pierce the cling film.
4. **I NEED** kitchen towels ("KT") to line a plate and/or to cover food.
5. **I NEED** oven gloves and a mat.
6. **I NEED** microwave-safe bowls and jugs.
7. **I NEED** a wooden or plastic spoon and spatula.

What can I ... should I ... use?

1. **I CAN USE** any glass utensils that have no metal trim. I can use Pyrex for microwave and grill.
2. **I CAN USE** all types of china that have no metal trim.
3. **I CAN USE** Polypropylene (microwave-safe plastic!) jugs for almost anything.
4. **I SHOULD USE** wooden skewers for kebabs – remember, no metal!
5. **I SHOULD USE** a browning dish to brown food.

codebreakers...

 help!

 cooking time

 cooking time

 cooking time

 rack and base cooking time

 help!!

 cooking time

 standing time

 browning time, covered

 "KT" lined plate cooking time

 help!!!

 cooking time

 cooking time

 browning time, uncovered

 covered plate cooking time

 preparation time

 standing time

 standing time

 standing time

 lined & covered cooking time

 red = FULL (100%)

 cooking time

 cooking time

 grilling time

 now clean up!

 orange = HIGH (70%)
yellow = MED (50%)

 standing time

 standing time

 potato standing time

 extra info

How to cover with cling film.

How to measure butter.

How to size an egg.

How to measure a spoonful.

How to avoid disaster.

How to curl a spring onion (see page 26).

How to add a drop of vanilla essence (see pages 40, 42 and 44).

How to make a chocolate cup case (see page 42).

...and cartoons

wrap a...

1 oz (25g) butter
1 corn on the cob
pinch of salt
pinch of paprika (optional)
small pinch garlic salt (optional)

1. Put the butter in a small bowl and cook for 1 minute.
2. Brush the corn with the melted butter and parcel in greaseproof paper, folding the ends tightly underneath so that the corn is completely sealed in.
3. Place in a dish. Cover with cling film, pierce and cook for 4 minutes.
4. Remove dish from oven and leave to stand for 1 minute. Then unwrap the corn carefully without spilling any of the melted butter. Spear the corn with corn holders and transfer to a plate.
5. Pour the butter back into the dish and throw away the greaseproof paper.
6. Add the salt – and the paprika and garlic salt if you are using them – to the melted butter and reheat for 30 seconds.
7. Pour the butter over the corn and away you go!

corn

1 egg
1 teaspoon cream or top of the milk
knob of butter
pinch of salt
1 grinding of black pepper
pinch of cayenne (optional – it's very hot!)
1 heaped tablespoon chopped ham
1 heaped tablespoon grated cheese
1 wholemeal roll
butter

scrambled egg

1. In a small bowl, beat the egg with a fork.
2. Add cream or top of the milk, butter, salt, pepper and cayenne (if you are using it).
3. Cook, uncovered, for 45 seconds on FULL (100%), stirring every 15 seconds.
4. Stir in ham and cheese and cook for a further 15 seconds.
5. Take out of the oven and quickly prepare the roll.

roll

1. Place roll on KT lined plate and heat through on MEDIUM (50%) for 30 seconds.
2. Cut in half and remove the soft inside.
3. Butter both halves. Pile egg onto bottom half and replace top of roll.
4. Take in both hands and . . . munch!

 If you prefer, scramble the egg without the ham and/or the cheese. The cooking time for the egg is still 1 minute.
Or try it on hot-buttered toast. Great for breakfast or supper.

egg

stack a...

1 pitta bread (wholemeal or white)
butter
2 slices of cooked ham
1 small tomato, sliced
4 heaped tablespoons grated cheese
slurp of sweetcorn relish (optional)
slurp of tomato ketchup (optional)

1. Place pitta on a rack and heat for ¾ minute on HIGH (70%). It will puff up while it heats.
2. Take it out and slit it down one side, or cut it in half, and butter the insides lightly.
3. Stack the ham, tomato slices and cheese inside, pushing well into the pocket.
4. Cook for 1 ½ minutes on HIGH (70%) till the cheese has melted.
5. If you like, add your relish and ketchup.

 Instead of using ham, make your stack with roast chicken or turkey or a cooked hamburger steak.
Try it with scrambled egg and bacon.
It's pretty good with mushrooms and cheese too!

pitta

make a...

knob of butter
4 oz (100g) beefburger
1 sesame bun
2 onion rings
2 slices tomato
1 slice processed cheese
1 lettuce leaf
your favourite relishes

1. Heat browning dish for 6 minutes. (⭐See maker's recommended time.)
2. Without removing dish from the oven, ⭐swirl the knob of butter round the dish.
3. Place the burger on the dish and press down hard with a wooden spatula to make sure that contact is made with the hot surface.
4. Cook for 1 ½ minutes on FULL (100%).
5. ⭐Turn over and cook the second side for 1 ½ minutes. (It will not be as brown as the first side, but it will be cooked.)
6. Cut bun in half and place bottom half on a KT lined plate. Build it up with onion rings, tomato, burger and, last of all, the slice of cheese.
7. Cook for 30 seconds (again on FULL) until the cheese has melted and is bubbling.
8. Add the top half of the bun and heat through on MEDIUM (50%) for 30 seconds.
9. Remove from the oven and pop a lettuce leaf inside.
10. Smother with your favourite relishes – ketchup, mustard, etc.

 If you don't like cheese – then make it without! It's easy. Just leave out instruction 7.

burger

top a...

basic tomato mixture

1 heaped tablespoon chopped onion
knob of butter
½ an 8 oz (225g) can of tomatoes,
drained and chopped

½ teaspoon tomato purée
pinch of dried basil and oregano
pinch of salt
1 grinding of black pepper

choose a base

1. 1 crumpet
2. 1 wholemeal muffin
3. 1 slice French bread, sliced long ways
4. 1 waffle

select your topping

1. 6 thin slices peperoni or spicy sausage
2. 2 anchovies, drained
2 pitted black olives, cut in half
3. 1 mushroom, thinly sliced
2 thin green pepper rings
2 stuffed olives, sliced
4. just tomato and cheese

which cheese?

1. 1 oz (25g) mozzarella, sliced
2. 2 heaped tablespoons grated Cheddar or gruyère cheese

1. Place chopped onion and a knob of butter in a bowl. Cover, pierce and cook for 1 ½ minutes.
2. Stir in drained and chopped tomatoes, tomato purée, basil and oregano (for that real Italian flavour), salt and pepper. Cover with a new piece of cling film, pierce and cook for 2 minutes.
3. Choose a base and brown it on both sides under a preheated conventional grill for 3 minutes, watching all the time.
4. Place base on a KT lined plate. Butter it and pile on tomato mixture, your favourite topping and finally the cheese and olives.
5. Cook for ¾ minute until the cheese has melted. Yummy.

pizza

colour some...

1 pint (600ml) boiling water
1 teaspoon salt
1 tablespoon vegetable oil
3 oz (75g) coloured pasta shapes
3 ½ oz (100g) jar ready-made tomato or bolognese sauce
1 heaped tablespoon grated parmesan cheese

1. ⭐Boil the water, pour it into the jug and add the salt and the oil.
2. Then add the pasta.
3. Cover, pierce and cook for 5 minutes.
4. Remove from oven and leave to stand for 5 minutes.
5. Meanwhile, place as much sauce as you want in a deep bowl.
6. Cover, pierce and cook for 1 ¼ minutes.
7. Drain pasta through a colander or sieve.
8. Tip onto a plate and pour the sauce over the top. Sprinkle with grated parmesan cheese.

 Spaghetti is not recommended as it is too long to fit in a jug of boiling water without burning your fingers!
Pasta comes in all shapes, sizes and colours. Try pink, green and white spirals (*fusilli*) or noodles (*tagliatelle* or *fettuccine*).

pasta

surprise a...

3 heaped tablespoons frozen mixed vegetables
½ tablespoon water
3 ½ oz (100g) can tuna, drained
3 level tablespoons condensed cream of chicken soup
½ teaspoon tomato purée
1 packet potato crisps
3 heaped tablespoons grated Cheddar or gruyère cheese

1. Place the vegetables and water in a bowl. Cover, pierce and cook for 1 ½ minutes. Drain thoroughly in a colander or sieve.
2. Flake the tuna with a fork.
3. Mix the soup and tomato purée in a small bowl.
4. Take a medium-sized bowl and put ½ the tuna in the bottom. Cover with ½ the soup mixture, then ½ the vegetables.
5. Repeat this with the rest of the tuna, soup and vegetables.
6. Cover, pierce and cook for 3 minutes.
7. Take out of the oven and stand for 1 minute.
8. Remove cling film and add enough crisps to cover the pie completely.
9. Top with the cheese.
10. Cook, uncovered, for 1 minute to allow the cheese to melt.

 You could always use prawns, canned salmon or diced cooked chicken instead of the tuna.

sailor

hash some...

½ oz (12½g) butter
2 heaped tablespoons chopped onion
4 oz (100g) cooked potatoes, diced
3 oz (75g) corned beef, chopped into cubes
1 teaspoon dried parsley
1 grinding of black pepper

1. Heat browning dish for 4 minutes. (⭐See maker's recommended time.)

2. ⭐ Place butter in dish and swirl round. Immediately, add onion and potatoes and press them down firmly with a wooden spatula to make contact with the bottom of the dish.

3. Cover with lid and cook for 1½ minutes.

4. Uncover, stir and again press down hard. Cook, uncovered, for 2 minutes.

5. Stir in corned beef, parsley and pepper. Cook for 3 more minutes, stirring after 1½ minutes.

6. Brown under preheated conventional grill for 4–6 minutes, watching all the time in case it starts to burn.

 To dice means to cut into small (dice-sized) cubes. Ordinary cubes are a little bigger!

stuff a...

1 medium potato
2 slices of bacon
knob of butter
½ tablespoon milk or cream
pinch of salt

1 grinding of black pepper
2 heaped tablespoons grated Cheddar
or gruyère cheese
1 heaped tablespoon baked beans –
barbecue flavour

1. Scrub and dry the potato, then prick it all over with a fork.
2. Place it on the rack and cook for 4 ½ minutes.
3. Turn potato over and cook for a further 4 ½ minutes.
4. Remove from oven ☆ using your oven gloves because the potato will be hot. Wrap it in a piece of aluminium foil.
5. Leave it to stand in its foil for 5 minutes.
6. Meanwhile, place the bacon on a KT lined plate and cover with another sheet of KT.
7. Cook for 1 minute. Turn bacon over, cover with the KT again and cook for 1 minute more.
8. Remove bacon from oven. Allow to cool for 1 minute. Break into small pieces with your fingers.
9. Unwrap potato and slice off the top.
10. With a spoon, carefully scoop out the inside of the potato into a bowl. (Don't tear the potato's jacket.) Mash the potato with a fork and add the butter, milk or cream, salt, pepper and cheese and mix well.
11. Gently stir the bacon pieces and baked beans into the mash. (Can you smell that barbecue?)
12. Fill the jacket with this dreamy mixture.
13. Place on the rack and cook for 1 ½ minutes to reheat.
14. Now enjoy your Baked Stuffed Potato – El Rancho!

potato

cap a...

1 spring onion (optional decoration)
1 large, very firm tomato
4 heaped tablespoons cooked turkey and stuffing
knob of butter
1 level tablespoon double cream
small pinch of dried parsley (optional)
2 heaped tablespoons grated Cheddar or gruyère cheese
pinch of salt
1 grinding of black pepper

1. First prepare your spring onion decoration as described on page 7.
2. Carefully cut the top off the tomato.
3. Use an apple corer to cut a hole in the centre of the tomato cap for the spring onion to go through.
4. Gently spoon out the inside of the tomato. You will not need this.
5. Place empty tomato and cap on a KT lined plate.
6. ☆Cut up turkey and stuffing into small pieces.
7. Place turkey, stuffing, butter, cream and parsley (if you are using it) in a bowl. Cover, pierce and cook for 1 ½ minutes.
8. Remove from the oven and stir in the cheese, salt and pepper.
9. Fill tomato with the mixture and cook for 30 seconds.
10. Place tomato cap on top and cook for a further 45 seconds.
11. Take your "curled" spring onion, dry it on "KT" and stick it, green side up, through the hole in the tomato cap. Very exotic!

 If you are not using the spring onion, don't make a hole in the tomato cap. Any Sunday roast leftovers will make a good stuffing for your tomato.

sail a...

1 medium-sized potato
2 tablespoons peas (fresh or frozen)
3 tablespoons chicken stock or water
2 teaspoons milk
½ oz (12½ g) butter
pinch of salt
1 grinding of black pepper
2 frankfurter sausages (thick, short variety)
2 heaped tablespoons Cheddar cheese (optional)
3 heaped tablespoons baked beans

green mash

1. ★Peel potato and cut into even sized chunks.
2. Place in a bowl with peas and chicken stock or water.
3. Cover, pierce and cook for 5 minutes.
4. Drain thoroughly. Return to the bowl, add milk, butter, salt and pepper and mash well with a fork.

boats

1. Prick sausages with a fork and put into a jug of hot, but not boiling, water.
2. Cook for 2 ½ minutes. Drain in a colander.
3. ★Make a deep slit lengthways in each sausage.
4. Fill slits with some of the mash. Don't overfill or they will capsize!
5. Top with half the cheese (if you are using it).
6. Spoon the beans onto a plate.
7. Carefully place sausage boats on top.
8. Surround with two scoops of mash (use an ice cream scoop if you have one) and pile the rest of the cheese on top.
9. Cook for 2 minutes to melt the cheese and heat the beans.

sausage

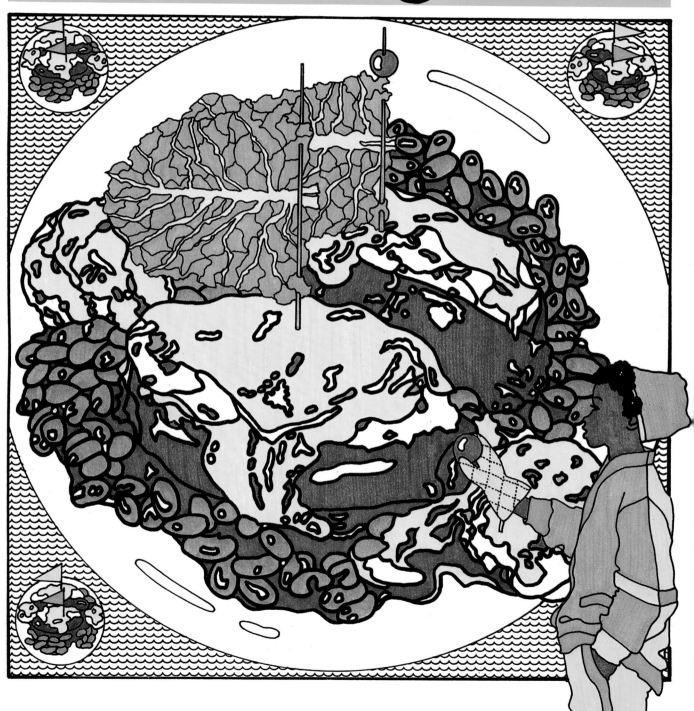

spear a...

4 oz (100g) chicken breast
2 small tomatoes, skins pierced
2 button mushrooms
4 "squares" of green pepper
2 thick slices of courgette

2 spring onions, white part only
vegetable oil
2 wooden skewers
1 wholemeal pitta bread
butter

1. Cut the chicken breast into 1 inch (2.5cm) cubes.
2. Wash and thoroughly dry the vegetables.
3. Put the chicken and vegetable pieces on the skewers, alternately.
4. Brush with a little vegetable oil.
5. Heat the browning dish for 4 minutes. (⭐See maker's recommended time.)
6. ⭐Remove the browning dish from the oven using your gloves and place it on a mat. Lay the loaded skewers inside the dish. With a spatula, press down hard on the skewers so that the food makes contact with the dish.
7. Cook for 1 ½ minutes on FULL (100%).
8. ⭐Remove from oven, turn skewers over and brush kebabs and vegetables with a little more oil. Press down hard with the spatula to make contact.
9. Cook for 2 minutes.
10. ⭐Remove from oven and stand for 2 minutes.
11. While the kebabs are "standing", place the pitta bread on the rack and cook on MEDIUM (50%) for 1 minute, turning over after 30 seconds.
12. Remove pitta from oven and slit open longways. Butter the inside and cook on MEDIUM (50%) for 30 seconds.
13. Fill pitta with kebabs.
14. With one hand lightly pressing on top of the pitta, carefully pull out the skewers.

 The kebabs will be really brown on one side only – but don't worry, the food will be cooked through.

kebab

fill some...

chilli

knob of butter
2 heaped tablespoons chopped onion
small pinch of garlic salt
1 ½ level tablespoons tomato purée
4 oz (100g) ground beef
1 heaped teaspoon chilli powder
pinch of oregano and cumin (optional)

2 ½ fl oz (75ml) hot water
¼ beef stock cube
4 heaped tablespoons canned, cooked red kidney beans, drained
1 grinding of black pepper
2 taco shells

decoration

½ avocado   1 tomato

1. Place butter, onion and garlic salt in a bowl. Cover, pierce and cook for 2 ½ minutes.
2. Remove from oven and stir in tomato purée. Cover (with a new piece of cling film if necessary and pierce) and cook for 1 minute.
3. Remove from oven, add beef, chilli powder and oregano and cumin (if you are using them). Stir well, cover and cook for 2 minutes.
4. Take out of the oven. Use a fork to break up the beef, cover and cook for 2 more minutes.
5. Mix the water with the stock cube.
6. Take the beef out of the oven and stir in the beef stock, beans and black pepper. Cover and cook for 3 minutes, stirring after 1 ½ minutes.
7. While the chilli is cooking, decorate your serving plate with a few avocado balls (scooped out with a melon baller) and a tomato cut in wedges. Very cool.
8. Remove chilli from oven and fill the taco shells.

 This recipe makes a mild chilli! Also try it with rice or a salad.

tacos

chop 'n...

rice

2 oz (50g) long grain rice
¼ chicken stock cube
¼ pint (150ml) boiling water

knob of butter
few natural roasted peanuts
(optional)

sauce

3 tablespoons Bramley apple sauce
1 tablespoon honey
1 tablespoon apple juice

pinch of salt
1 grinding of black pepper

chop

1 boneless pork chop
1 pineapple ring (fresh or canned)

1 cocktail cherry (optional)

1. Place rice in a large jug. Dissolve stock cube in boiling water. Pour over the rice.
2. Cover, pierce and cook for 7 minutes.
3. Stand for 5 minutes. All the water will be absorbed.
4. Mix sauce ingredients in a jug. Cover, pierce and cook for 1 minute.
5. Place chop in a small, shallow casserole. Pour sauce over. Cover, pierce and cook for 2 minutes.
6. Remove from oven, turn chop over. Cover and cook for 1 minute.
7. Remove from oven, turn chop over. Cover and cook for a further 1 minute.
8. Remove from oven and turn chop over again. Place pineapple ring on top. Cover and cook for 1 ½ minutes.
9. Stand for 2 minutes.

now put them together

1. Stir butter and peanuts (if you are using them) into the rice with a fork and dish up onto a plate.
2. Place the pork chop with the pineapple ring on the pile of rice and spoon over the sauce. Stick a cherry on top.

stir fry...

select 4–5 oz (100–130g) vegetables from

1 carrot, scraped and cut into thin ribbons with a potato peeler	1 small courgette, thinly sliced
3–4 broccoli or cauliflower fleurets	3–4 baby corn, fresh or canned
	2 button mushrooms, sliced
	3 squares of green pepper

plus

½ teaspoon vegetable or sesame oil	5–6 mange tout, trimmed at both ends
½ teaspoon water	4 heaped tablespoons fresh bean sprouts
3 drops of soy sauce	
2 spring onions, sliced	1 ½ teaspoons bottled oyster sauce

1. Wash, dry and cut vegetables as instructed above. (★Help cutting please!)

2. Heat browning dish for 4 minutes. (★See maker's recommended time.)

3. Remove from oven and ★swirl the oil round to coat the dish. Immediately add your selection of vegetables and keep stirring until the dish cools slightly (about ½ minute).

4. Add water and soy sauce. Cover with lid and cook for ½ minute.

5. Remove from oven and stir in spring onion, mange tout, bean sprouts and oyster sauce.

6. Cover and cook for ½ minute.

7. Have your bowl and chopsticks ready . . . Serve immediately!

 You may like to add a few shelled peanuts, cashew nuts or toasted almonds just before serving.

crunch a...

1 cooking apple, approx 6 oz (170g)
1 ½ sweetmeal digestive biscuits
1 heaped tablespoon soft brown sugar
½ oz (12½g) butter
4 rounded tablespoons hazelnut yogurt
few chopped nuts
1 glacé cherry (green or red) to decorate

1. ☆ Peel and core the apple and slice thinly.
2. Place in a small dessert dish and cook for 3 minutes.
3. Crumble the biscuits and mix with the sugar.
4. Cover the cooked apple with the biscuit crumb mixture.
5. Place butter in a small bowl and cook for 1 minute.
6. Pour butter evenly over the biscuit mixture and cook for 3 minutes.
7. Remove from the oven carefully – it will be hot because of the sugar content – and stand for 3 minutes.
8. Spoon the yogurt over the top and decorate with the chopped nuts.
9. Add a cherry in the middle.
10. If you like it hot, eat the crunch immediately. It's also yummy cold. Just refrigerate for an hour to chill it.

 You can use any 1-portion glass, pyrex, china or plastic dessert dish but ☆ you must be sure it's microwave-safe!

butter a...

1 ½ oz (40g) butter
3 thin slices white bread
1 heaped tablespoon sultanas or currants
1 egg
2 fl oz (50ml) milk
1 level tablespoon double cream
1 heaped tablespoon caster sugar
2 drops vanilla essence (see page 7)

1. Cook a knob of the measured butter in the pie dish for 30 seconds.
2. Use a pastry brush to grease the pie dish with the softened butter.
3. Cut the crusts off the bread and butter both sides, using up all the remaining butter.
4. Using 1 ½ slices of bread, cover the bottom of the pie dish. Trim the bread to fit the dish.
5. Sprinkle ½ the sultanas or currants on top.
6. Cover with the remaining bread, trimming as before. Cover with the rest of the sultanas or currants.
7. ⭐ Whisk egg until foaming.
8. Pour in milk, cream, sugar and vanilla essence and whisk it all together for a few seconds.
9. Pour evenly over the bread and leave for about 10 minutes so that the bread can absorb most of the liquid.
10. Cook for 3 minutes, turning the pie dish around every minute so that it cooks evenly. Watch the bread puff up as it goes round!
11. Remove from oven, ⭐ remembering to use gloves as it will be hot, and stand on a mat for 3 minutes.
12. Heat the conventional grill while the pudding is standing.
13. Brown under the grill for 2 or 3 minutes.

 Save the crusts from the bread for the wild birds!

pudding

serve a...

1 ½ oz (40g) white chocolate
2 paper cup cases
2 oz (50g) plain block chocolate
2 teaspoons black coffee
knob of butter

1 drop vanilla essence (see page 7)
1 egg
squirt of aerosol cream
1 "Smarty"

white chocolate cup case
1. Break white chocolate into pieces and place in a small bowl.
2. Cook for 2 minutes. Stir. Cook for 1 ½ minutes. Remove from oven.
3. Fit one paper cup case inside the other (for strength) and turn to page 7 for detailed instructions, comic strip style.

meanwhile . . . make the mousse
1. Break the plain chocolate into pieces and place in a small bowl with the coffee.
2. Cook for ½ minute. Stir. Cook for a further ¼ minute.
3. Remove from oven and stir in the butter and vanilla essence.
4. ★ Separate the egg into 2 bowls. (Be sure there's no yolk in the white part!)
5. Mix the yolk into the chocolate mixture, stirring well.
6. ★ Whisk the egg white until stiff, using an electric whisk.
7. Gently stir it into the chocolate mixture.
8. Fill the white chocolate cup case with the mousse.
9. Place on a small plate and refrigerate until the mousse has set. (About 30 minutes.)

decoration
1. Remove mousse from the refrigerator just before you are going to eat it and squirt a little cream on top.
2. Add your "Smarty" in the centre of the cream. Yummmmmmm. .y!

mousse

crack a...

3 drops vanilla essence (see page 7)
½ level teaspoon bicarbonate of soda
½ teaspoon cold water
6 rounded tablespoons demerara sugar
2½ heaped tablespoons golden syrup

1 tablespoon water
½ oz (12½g) butter
3 oz (75g) dry roasted peanuts
vegetable oil, to grease palette knife

1. Mix vanilla, bicarbonate of soda and ½ teaspoon of cold water in a small bowl and put on one side until needed.
2. Place sugar, syrup and water in a large 3½ pint (2 litre) jug and cook for 2 minutes.
3. ★Remove from oven, using gloves – because the sugar will make it very hot – and put on a mat. Stir well, add butter and cook for 1 minute. Remove from oven and stir again.
4. Add peanuts – but do not stir! Cook for 2½ minutes.
5. Be very careful! ★Use gloves to remove bowl from oven!
6. Add prepared vanilla mixture to bowl and stir with a wooden spoon for 1 minute.
7. Line a baking tray with greaseproof paper and pour mixture onto this.
8. Smooth over and flatten the mixture to a depth of about ¼ inch (6mm) with a lightly oiled palette knife.
9. Cover with another sheet of greaseproof paper. Grip the edges of the greaseproof and turn the mixture over.
10. Leave mixture between greaseproof paper to cool (about 2 minutes).
11. ★"Stretch" the mixture in all directions with your hands until quite thin. (It stretches very easily at this stage!)
12. When it is quite cold, break into pieces. And if there is any left, store it in an airtight glass jar. It will stay crunchy for weeks.

 Perhaps one for the adults to try first.

44

peanut

ice hot...

2 heaped teaspoons cocoa powder
1 heaped teaspoon caster sugar
½ pint (300ml) milk
1 scoop chocolate ice cream
aerosol cream (plain or chocolate flavoured)
chocolate chips

1. In a large jug mix cocoa powder and sugar with 1 tablespoon of the milk until it's a smooth paste.

2. Heat the rest of the milk in a second jug for 3 minutes.

3. Gradually pour the milk into the cocoa mixture, stirring all the time.

4. Beat with a wire whisk till bubbles form.

5. Reheat for 1 minute. Whisk again.

6. Pour into mug or heatproof glass.

7. Add 1 scoop of ice cream.

8. Squirt cream on top.

9. Drop a few chocolate chips onto the cream and eat it before the ice cream melts. Hmmmmm . . . Real dreamy stuff!

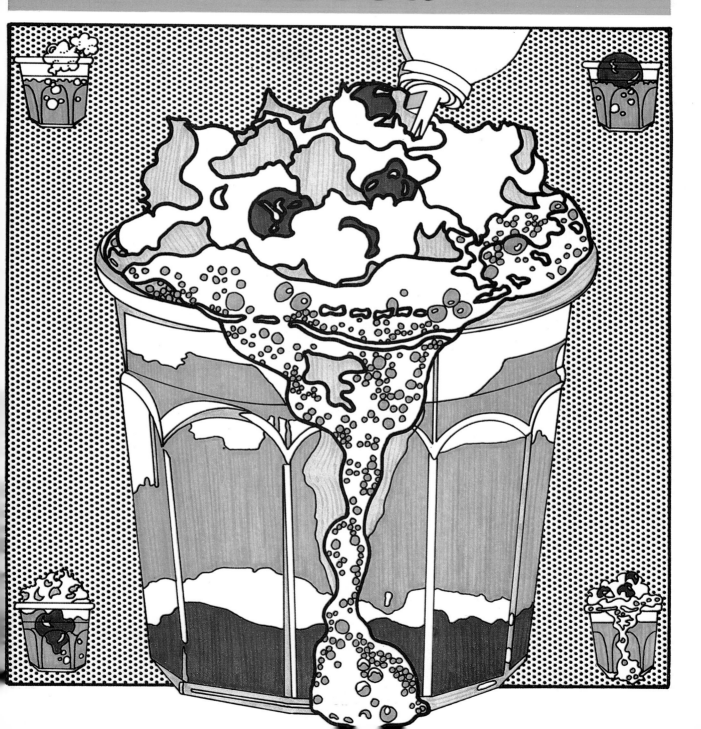